Dear Parents and Educators,

Welcome to Penguin Young Readers! As parents and educators, you know that each child develops at his or her own pace—in terms of speech, critical thinking, and, of course, reading. Penguin Young Readers recognizes this fact. As a result, each Penguin Young Readers book is assigned a traditional easy-to-read level (1–4) as well as a Guided Reading Level (A–P). Both of these systems will help you choose the right book for your child. Please refer to the back of each book for specific leveling information. Penguin Young Readers features esteemed authors and illustrators, stories about favorite characters, fascinating nonfiction, and more!

The Moon

LEVEL **4**

GUIDED READING LEVEL **O**

This book is perfect for a **Fluent Reader** who:
• can read the text quickly with minimal effort;
• has good comprehension skills;
• can self-correct (can recognize when something doesn't sound right); and
• can read aloud smoothly and with expression.

Here are some **activities** you can do during and after reading this book:
• Comprehension: After reading the book, answer the following questions:
  • How long does it take the Moon to go around the Earth?
  • Who was one of the first scientists to observe the Moon through a telescope?
  • Why do we always see the same side of the Moon?
  • Does the Moon change shape? If not, why does it look different at different times?
  • What is it called when Earth blocks light from the Sun from reaching the Moon?
• Research: The Moon orbits the Earth. But other planets have moons, too. Research another planet in our solar system. Does it have an orbiting moon? How is that moon like ours?

Remember, sharing the love of reading with a child is the best gift you can give!

—Bonnie Bader, EdM
   Penguin Young Readers program

*Penguin Young Readers are leveled by independent reviewers applying the standards developed by Irene Fountas and Gay Su Pinnell in *Matching Books to Readers: Using Leveled Books in Guided Reading*, Heinemann, 1999.

PENGUIN YOUNG READERS
An Imprint of Penguin Random House LLC

● Smithsonian

This trademark is owned by the Smithsonian Institution and is registered in the U.S. Patent and Trademark Office.

Smithsonian Enterprises:
Christopher Liedel, President
Carol LeBlanc, Senior Vice President, Education and Consumer Products
Brigid Ferraro, Vice President, Education and Consumer Products
Ellen Nanney, Licensing Manager
Kealy Gordon, Product Development Manager

Andrew K. Johnston, Geographer, Center for Earth and Planetary Studies,
National Air and Space Museum, Smithsonian

Photo credits: NASA: pages 4 (photo by Dominic Milan), 9, 18, 19, 20–21, 22, 23, 24, 25, 26 (photo by Stephen J. Edberg), 32, 33, 35, 36–37, 39, 40, 41, 42, 43, 44, 45, 46–47.
NASA/EDO: page 27.
NASA/JPF: page 29. Smithsonian Institution Libraries: pages 11, 17.
Smithsonian National Air & Space Museum: pages 38, 42.
Smithsonian National Museum of the American Indian: page 8.
Thinkstock: pages 3, 48 (© Gregor Kervina), 6 (© Ingram Publishing), 12, 16 (© Karen Faljyan), 13 (© Crossy 2009), 15 (© sergeyussr 2009), 30–31 (© DmitriyBurlakov).

Library of Congress Cataloging-in-Publication Data is available.

ISBN 978-0-448-49020-5 (pbk)   10 9 8 7 6 5 4 3 2 1
ISBN 978-0-448-49021-2 (hc)   10 9 8 7 6 5 4 3 2 1

Smithsonian

THE MOON

by James Buckley Jr.

Penguin Young Readers
An Imprint of Penguin Random House

Contents

Look Up!

    People have looked up at the Moon for thousands and thousands of years. No matter where you are on Earth, you can see it. The Moon travels around the Earth. Together, the Earth and the Moon travel around the Sun. The Moon is a part of our sky and our lives.

    Let's meet our closest neighbor in space!

From the beginning, people wondered, "What is the Moon?" They answered that question with stories that have been handed down over many, many years.

In some American Indian stories, the Moon helped create the universe and life on Earth.

Long ago the Greeks, the Romans, and the Chinese honored a moon goddess.

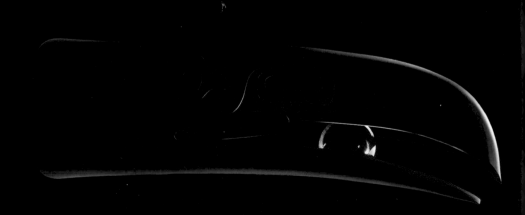

The moon goddess Chang'e

The Tlingit people of Alaska tell of a chief who held the Sun and the Moon in boxes. Raven set them free. Then there was light, day, and night.

An English folktale says that the Moon is made of green cheese.

Have you heard of the "Man in the Moon"? There are many stories about this "face" on the Moon's surface.

The Moon has also inspired writers. The famous French author Jules Verne wrote *From the Earth to the Moon* in 1865. But by that time, we had learned many facts about the Moon.

Keeping Time

Early Moon watchers saw that the Moon appeared to rise and set. They also noticed that it appeared to change shape. People saw that these events happened in a **pattern**. The Moon changed the same way, time after time.

Since people long ago did not
have clocks, they **observed** the world
around them to keep track of time.
One of the best ways to keep time
was to watch the Moon.

The Moon takes about 29 days to go around the Earth once. Those 29 days came to be called a month.

People began to break up each year into how many times the Moon went through this pattern. The 12 times the Moon changed became the 12 months of the year.

A moon chart from 1708

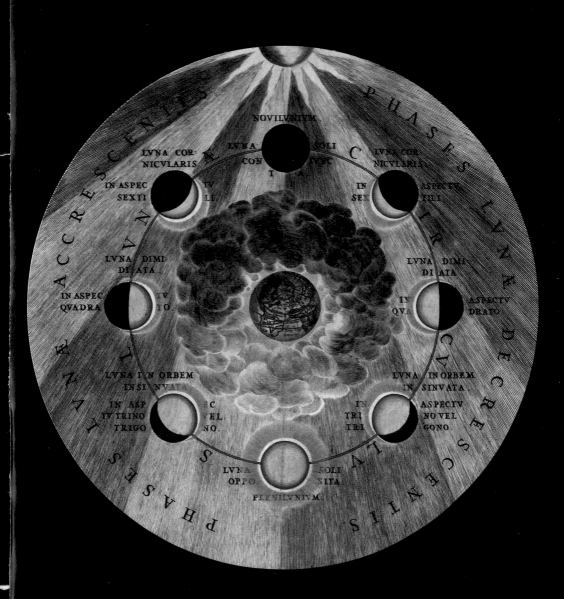

A Closer Look

How did people first look at the Moon? They used their eyes, of course!

But some people wanted a closer look, so in the 1600s, they developed telescopes. An Italian scientist of that time named Galileo Galilei built a telescope. He could see the Moon close-up with it.

The Moon had an uneven surface. Some areas were rough, and some were smooth. Galileo and other scientists began to study the Moon closely.

Over time, people built bigger and bigger telescopes. They spied huge craters, hills, and mountains on the Moon. But there was no "Man in the Moon." In fact, there were no signs of life.

Today, the most important
telescope is not even on Earth.
The Hubble Space Telescope orbits
Earth like the Moon does. It has
taken amazing photos of the Moon
from space.

Not Cheese!

Looking through all those telescopes proved that the Moon isn't green or cheesy!

The Moon is really made from rock. Scientists say the Moon was formed more than 4 billion years ago.

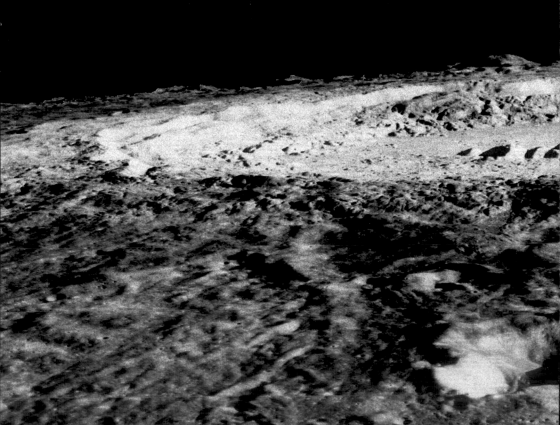

An object as big as Mars smashed into the Earth. Pieces of this space object and the Earth broke off in the impact. This **debris** floated around the Earth. Over time, the pieces came together to form the Moon.

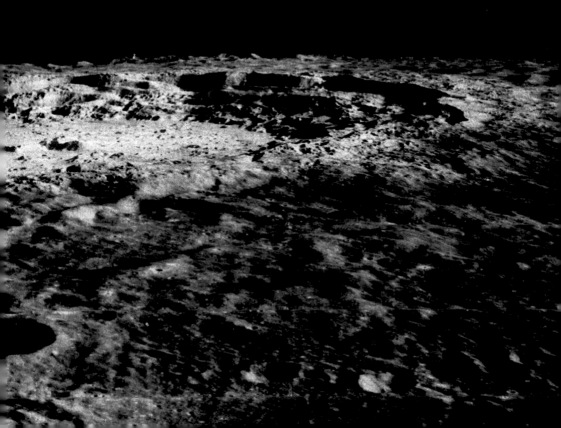

The Moon in Motion

The Moon's path around the Earth is called an **orbit**. The Moon also spins like a top as it orbits Earth. That's why we always see the same side of the Moon.

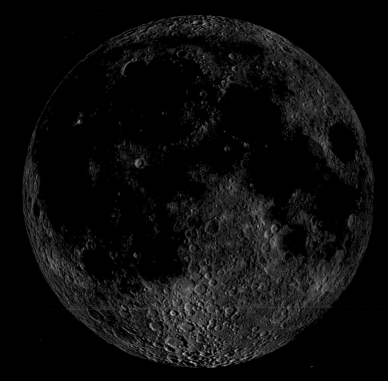

The near side of the Moon

The Moon takes about 29 days to spin around once, the same as it takes to orbit the Earth once.

The far side of the Moon

Why does the Moon change shape?

It doesn't!

What changes is how much of the Moon is hit by the Sun's light. The Moon does not make light. It shines by reflecting light from the Sun.

As the Moon orbits, a different part is lit each night. That's why it appears to change shape over a month.

This pattern is called the **phases** of the Moon.

Hide-and-Seek Moon

Sometimes, the Earth comes between the Sun and the Moon. Our planet blocks the Sun's light from hitting the Moon for a few minutes. This is called a **lunar** eclipse. **Lunar** means "having to do with the Moon."

Lunar eclipse

Other times, the Moon blocks the Sun's rays from the Earth. This is called a **solar** eclipse. **Solar** means "having to do with the Sun."

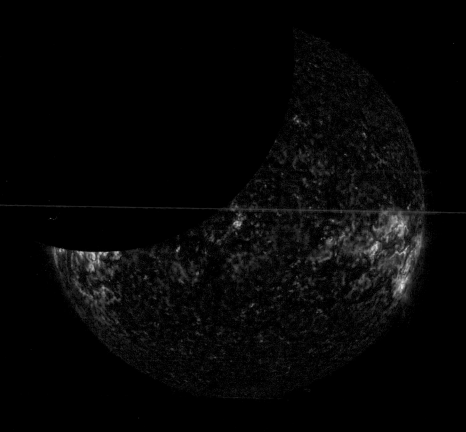

Solar eclipse

Tides

Gravity is the force that holds us on Earth. Gravity also keeps Earth in orbit around the Sun. It keeps the Moon spinning around Earth, too.

Gravity works both ways. **Gravitational** pull from the Moon reaches the Earth. The Moon's gravity creates a daily change in the world's oceans.

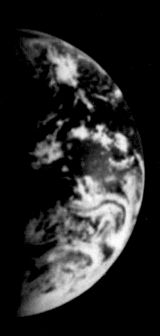

The Moon in orbit around Earth

The gravity of the Moon pulls the oceans toward the Moon itself. The water **bulges** toward the Moon. As the Moon orbits, the bulge in the oceans moves with it.

That movement is called the **tide**.
The tide comes in and out twice
a day where oceans meet land—
thanks to the Moon!

The Real Men on the Moon

Studying the Moon from afar was not enough. People wanted to *go* there.

In the 1950s, new rockets were built. Soon, the United States and the Soviet Union each launched people into space with these powerful machines.

Yuri Gagarin of the Soviet Union, the first human in space

In 1961, the president of the United States, John F. Kennedy, set a goal: reach the Moon itself by 1969. The space race was on!

President John F. Kennedy

In the early 1960s, the United States sent the Mercury **astronauts** into space. They orbited the Earth and learned about space travel.

The Mercury missions were practice for traveling to the Moon.

John Glenn squeezes into the Mercury Friendship 7 **capsule**. He became the first American to orbit the Earth.

A later space program was called Apollo, after the Greek god of the Sun. These spaceflights used even larger rockets. Some of them sent people into orbit around the Moon for the first time.

Each Apollo mission was given a number. During Apollo 8, the astronauts took some famous photos.

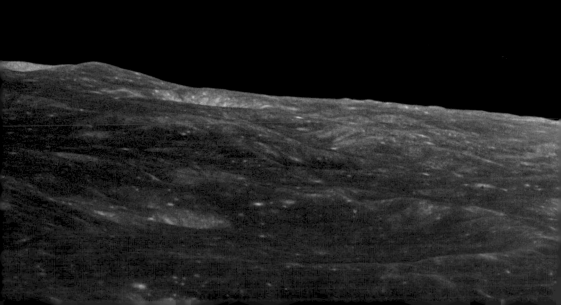

For the first time in human history, we were able to see what our planet looked like from the Moon!

Earth rise

Now it was time to win the space race! Apollo 11 launched on July 16, 1969. On board were astronauts Neil Armstrong, Edwin "Buzz" Aldrin, and Michael Collins.

It took Apollo 11 three days to reach the Moon. Armstrong and Aldrin landed a lunar craft on the Moon's surface. Collins stayed on board the spacecraft to pick up the other two.

Apollo 11 cuff links

Apollo 11 patch

Apollo 11 checklist

Blast off, Apollo 11

On July 20, Neil Armstrong became the first human to step onto the Moon. His words are famous:

"One small step for a man, one giant leap for mankind."

Neil Armstrong

The flag and a TV camera

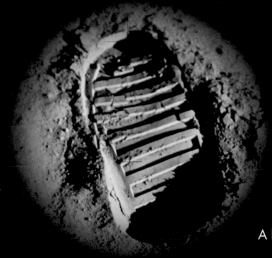

A bootprint that is still there!

Beyond Apollo 11

Apollo 11's crew were welcomed back to Earth as heroes.

Even though they had landed on the Moon, the Apollo space program continued. Apollo 12's astronauts dug up lunar soil. They gathered about 70 pounds of Moon rocks. Scientists on Earth studied what they brought back.

Lunar soil sample

Apollo 13's astronauts didn't make it to the Moon. They almost didn't make it back to Earth!

A dangerous problem arose on the moving spacecraft. The Apollo 13 crew and mission control on Earth had a tense few days to deal with. The astronauts barely returned safely.

The Apollo 13 crew after their capsule splashed down

The troubles with Apollo 13 didn't stop the space program, though. On the next mission, Apollo 14 astronaut Alan Shepard brought a golf club with him. He hit the first golf ball on the Moon!

Alan Shepard

Astronauts on Apollo 15 didn't just walk on the Moon—they drove! A special **lunar rover** was built to help them explore larger areas. Crews on Apollo 16 and 17 used the rover as well.

Apollo 17 was the last time that human beings visited the Moon . . . so far!

The lunar rover, Apollo 17

People are still exploring the Moon with spacecraft. These **robotic** spacecraft circle the Moon and take photographs. Scientists are even discussing building bases on the Moon.

Our Moon is not the only moon in the solar system. Scientists have counted 145 moons around the eight planets.

Could there be other life in the universe? Do you think they look up at their own moons like we do?

Artwork of some moons in our solar system

Glossary

astronaut: a person who travels to space

bulges: expands and changes shape

capsule: the part of a rocket that carries the astronauts

debris: broken parts of a whole

gravitational: having to do with gravity, the force that holds objects to Earth or other bodies in space

lunar: having to do with the Moon

lunar rover: a four-wheel electric vehicle driven on the Moon

observed: looked at over time

orbit: the path of one object in space around another

pattern: something that repeats in an order

phases: the different ways that the Moon appears to people on Earth as a month goes by

robotic: having to do with robots; powered by robot technology

solar: having to do with the Sun or sunlight

tide: the twice-daily flow of ocean water toward and away from a shore